Michael McClure's *The Beard* is a mysterious piece of work, for while its surface seems simple, repetitive and obscene, there is an action working which is dramatic and comic at once, and the play emits an odd but intense field of attention, almost like a magnetic field, almost as if ghosts from two periods of the American past were speaking across decades to each other, and yet at the same time are present in our living room undressing themselves or speaking to us of the nature of seduction, the nature of attraction, and particularly, the nature of perverse temper between a man and a woman. Obstinacy face to face with the sly feint and parry all in one, the repitition serves almost as subway stops on that electric trip a man and a woman make if they move from the mind to the flesh. That mysterious trip, whose mystery often resides in the dilema of whether the action is extraordinarily serious or meaningless. It is with these ambiguities, these effervescences, that *The Beard* plays, masterfully, be it said, like a juggler.

Norman Mailer

THE BEARD

MICHAEL McCLURE

THE BEARD

COYOTE : 1967

a COYOTE book, published by James Koller
distributed by City Lights Books,
261 Columbus Ave., San Francisco, California 94111

Edition limited to 5000 copies
of which 40 are specially bound
and signed.

First Printing, March 1967

Book design by Dave Haselwood
Cover design by Wes Wilson
Cover photo of Billie Dixon and Richard Bright by
Clark Worswick

THE BEARD

HARLOW and BILLY THE KID wear small beards of torn white tissue paper.

HARLOW'S hair is in her traditional style. She wears a pale blue gown with plumed sleeves.

BILLY THE KID wears shirt, tight pants, and boots.

HARLOW has a purse.

The set contains two chairs and a table covered with furs — there is an orange light shining on them.

The Beard was performed for the first time on December 18, 1965 at the Actor's Workshop in San Francisco. The play was directed by Marc Estrin. The set was designed by Robert LaVigne and costumes were designed by Louise Foss. The cast was as follows:

Jean Harlow . . . . Billie Dixon
Billy the Kid . . . . Richard Bright

The Beard was first published in a presentation edition of 300 copies. The author wishes to extend his special thanks to Billie Dixon, Richard Bright, Marc Estrin, Robert LaVigne, and Marshall Krause of the ACLU — for all we have gone through together to make a blue velvet eternity.

THE BEARD

HARLOW: Before you can pry any secrets from me, you must first find the real me! Which one will you pursue?

THE KID: What makes you think I want to pry secrets from you?

HARLOW: Because I'm so beautiful.

THE KID: So what!

HARLOW: You want to be as beautiful as I am.

THE KID: Oh yeah!

HARLOW: Before you can pry any secrets from me, you must first find the real me! Which one will you pursue?

THE KID: What makes you think I want to pry secrets from you?

HARLOW: Because I'm so beautiful.

THE KID: So what!

HARLOW: You want to be as beautiful as I am.

THE KID: Oh yeah! *(Pause. He grabs her arm.)*
I'VE GOT YOU!

HARLOW: It's an illusion!

THE KID: *(Squeezing her arm and raising it)* You mean
this meat isn't you?

HARLOW: What do you think?

THE KID: What makes you think you're so beautiful?

HARLOW: Oh, my thighs . . . my voice . . .

THE KID: What about your hair . . . ?

HARLOW: What do you think?

THE KID: Your hair came out of a bottle.

HARLOW: You're full of shit! My hair is beautiful and it
didn't come out of any bottle — it's like this.

THE KID: Show me your baby pictures!

HARLOW: You're crazy! Why?

THE KID: To see your hair!

HARLOW: You ARE jealous.

THE KID: You're full of shit!

HARLOW: It's blond — don't worry! You've got buck teeth!

THE KID: SHUT UP!

HARLOW: You'd like to be beautiful! Maybe you'd even like to be pretty. You wear your hair down to your shoulders. Maybe you'd like to be a chick!

THE KID: (*He takes hold of her arm — rolls it in his fingers*) THIS IS NOTHING BUT MEAT! (*He sneers*)

HARLOW: Before you can pry any secrets from me, you must first find the real me!

THE KID: What makes you think I want to pry secrets from you?

HARLOW: Because I'm so beautiful.

THE KID: So what!

HARLOW: You want to be as beautiful as I am!

THE KID: Oh yeah!
        THIS IS NOTHING BUT MEAT! (*He squeezes her bare arm and rolls it in his fingers.*) —Why should I want to be beautiful?

11

HARLOW: Oh . . . You're a man.

THE KID: Yeah?

HARLOW: You're a man... And men want to be beautiful.

THE KID: I'm sick of that word . . it makes me want to puke!
YOU'RE A BAG OF MEAT!

HARLOW: What word?

THE KID: *Beautiful.* I'm sick of hearing that word coming from a bag of meat.

HARLOW: Don't touch my arm again!

THE KID: Or?

HARLOW: I'll cut your dumb brain open like a bag of meat!
— Don't you think I'm . . . lovely . . .

THE KID: You smell like myrrh. Come and sit on my lap. (*He pulls her arm*)

HARLOW: What if somebody came in and looked!

THE KID: In eternity. —There's nobody here!

HARLOW: You said I'm a bag of meat! And you said shit about my hair!

THE KID: Maybe I love you.

HARLOW: You're full of shit. WHO CAN LOVE IN ETERNITY?

THE KID: (*With sureness*) Sit on my lap.

HARLOW: You're a million miles away, Sweet.

THE KID: Not in eternity! . . . Sit on my lap!

HARLOW: FUCK YOU!

THE KID: YOU'RE A BAG OF MEAT! A white sack of soft skin and fat held in shape by a lot of bones!

HARLOW: (*Pulling dress up thigh*) So?

THE KID: (*Suddenly*) I think your hair's blond!

HARLOW: Really blond?

THE KID: Yes!

HARLOW: You're a sack of shit!

THE KID: Sit on my lap!

HARLOW: Before you can pry any secrets from me, you must first find the real me! Which one will you pursue?

THE KID: What makes you think I want to pry secrets from you?

HARLOW: Because I'm beautiful.

13

THE KID: So what!

HARLOW: You want to be as beautiful as I am!

THE KID: Oh yeah! Come here, and sit on my lap and lick my boots!

HARLOW: You're full of shit! You wish you were a chick!

THE KID: Come here, and sit on my lap. I'll let you lick my boots.

HARLOW: Why should I lick your boots?

THE KID: You'd love to!

HARLOW: Before you can pry any . . .

THE KID: SHUT UP!

HARLOW: You'd like to grab my blond hair in your hands?

THE KID: So what!

HARLOW: You'd like to see me crawl?

THE KID: (*Shrugs*)

HARLOW: Why should I lick your boots?

THE KID: (*Shrugs*) Come here and sit on my lap then.

HARLOW: Why do you want me to lick your boots?

THE KID: I'd like to make speeches like big thick clouds.

HARLOW: You will, Baby, you will.

THE KID: What if I talk like this — NICE AND LOUD!

HARLOW: You want me to lick your boots, huh? That's no way to steal beauty, Kid.

THE KID: Maybe I'll take your blond hair in my hands.

HARLOW: Why don't you, Kid?

THE KID: Come here and sit on my lap and lick my hands.

HARLOW: Why don't you take me by the hair then?

THE KID: Maybe I will.
Come over here and sit on my lap, Babe.

HARLOW: One chick on another chick's lap! You're full of shit!

THE KID: Before you can pry any secrets out of me, you must first find the real me! Which one will you pursue?

HARLOW: What makes you think I want to pry secrets from you?

THE KID: Because I'm beautiful.

HARLOW: So what?

THE KID: You want to be as beautiful as I am.

HARLOW: You're nothing but meat pushed into a bag of skin with buck teeth and long hair. —And you want *me* to kiss YOUR boots.

THE KID: Come here and sit on my lap and I'll let you hold my cock.

HARLOW: Now wouldn't I like THAT! —A chunk of meat hanging from a hunk of meat!

THE KID: And afterwards you can lick my boots! (—Which one of me will you pursue?) Maybe you'll find I'm sheer spirit taking the guise of meat.

HARLOW: What makes you think I'd want to lick YOUR boots?

THE KID: Because there are rainbows on them! Rainbows reflected on sheer black.

HARLOW: Let me see.

THE KID: (*Holds his boots in the light*)

HARLOW: They're not bad.

THE KID: Come and sit on my lap.

HARLOW: You're a cunt!

THE KID: Sit on my lap.

HARLOW: And you'll take my blond hair in your crumby hands! Why should I lick your boots or sit on your lap?

THE KID: There's nobody here.

HARLOW: Why should I lick your boots or sit on your lap?

THE KID: THERE'S NOBODY HERE!

HARLOW: Nobody to see, you mean? Huh?

THE KID: That's right. There's nobody here. Sit on my lap.

HARLOW: What if I DID?

THE KID: You could lick my boots then . . . and touch my cock!

HARLOW: You must first find the real me! Which one will you pursue?

THE KID: There's only one you!

HARLOW: You're full of shit! O.K., I'm sick of this! What do you want?

THE KID: I want you to sit on my lap and touch my cock.

HARLOW: I don't give a fuck where we are . . . I'm sick

of this talk!

THE KID: Then shut up! You started it!

HARLOW: What I said was: Before you can pry any secrets out of me, you must first find the real me! Which one will you pursue?

THE KID: I'm sick of this shit too! It's a fucking rite! It makes me think of one of those steel black wasps crawling over black velvet.

HARLOW: And I suppose you're soft and real!

THE KID: FUCK YOU!

HARLOW: I'm real *wherever* I am!

THE KID: (*Sneering*) Well, I'm real too.

HARLOW: Your eyes are crazier than Hell! They stare! You're out of your mind! Before you can pry any secrets out of me, you must first find the real me! Which one will you pursue?

THE KID: I wouldn't follow you across an empty street.

HARLOW: Well, you're HERE!

THE KID: You're here too!
You say you're an illusion — and there's more than one you! And you say my eyes are crazy! SHOVE OFF!

HARLOW: (*Stands. Looks around.*) There's nothing here but blue velvet!

THE KID: Yeah. (*Smiling, crossing leg*)

(*HARLOW walks around stroking the velvet. Pauses. Adjusts herself in the chair sexually.*)

THE KID: What makes you say my eyes are crazy?

HARLOW: I DON'T WANT TO TALK ABOUT IT. (*Pause*) Why do you say I'm an illusion?

THE KID: You said it, not me!

HARLOW: Yeah. (*Thinking*)
(*Pause*)
Your eyes are crazy because you're full of shit, Sweetie.

THE KID: I despise dirty mouthed chicks.

HARLOW: Let's be clean . . .

THE KID: O. k.

(*Pause*)

HARLOW: (*Angrily*) FUCK YOU!

(*Pause. KID takes out handkerchief and polishes toes of his boots*)

FUCK YOU! FUCK YOU! FUCK YOU!

(Pause. KID polishes toes of his boots.)

FUCK YOU! FUCK YOU! OHHhhh FUCK
YOU!

THE KID: And you say I'm crazy.

HARLOW: You're crazier than Hell, you frozen eyed
bastard!

THE KID: Can't you be clean?

HARLOW: How about you?

THE KID: *(Shrugs. Holds up his boot)* How about that!

HARLOW: You make me sick talking about your lap and
your boots!

THE KID: And my cock?

HARLOW: That too! And calling me a bag of meat!

THE KID: You said you were an illusion!

HARLOW: Fuck you!

THE KID: And you called me dumb and crazy.

HARLOW: That was way back then in the rite.

THE KID: Everything is NOW.

HARLOW: You ARE crazy! (*Curls up in chair*) I'm going
to sleep . . .

THE KID: In eternity?

HARLOW: Skip it! (*Makes herself more comfortable*)

(*Pause*)

THE KID: Hey!

HARLOW: I'm asleep!

THE KID: Come and sit on my lap.

(*No action*)

Hey!

(*No action*)

Hey!

HARLOW: (*Leaping up*) YOU'RE OUT OF YOUR MIND!

THE KID: In eternity? (*Squinting*) How can I be out of
my mind in eternity?

HARLOW: If eternity is blue velvet it's a bunch of shit!
(*Paces*)

THE KID: Maybe it's not!

HARLOW: (*Pacing*) Not what?

THE KID: Velvet! (*Watches her pace*)
Sit down!

HARLOW: WHAT?

THE KID: Sit down.

HARLOW: (*Angrily*) In your lap?

THE KID: (*Quietly and firmly with a gesture*) Sit down.

(*HARLOW sits back in chair. —They stare at each other.*)

HARLOW: (*Enticingly*) Before you can pry any secrets from me, you must first find the real me! Which one will you pursue?

THE KID: SHUT UP!

HARLOW: Before you can pry any . . .

THE KID: (*Leaping up as if to strike her*) SHUT UP!!

HARLOW: Before you can pry any . . .

THE KID: (*Raising hand to strike her*) SHUT UP!! SHUT UP!! GOD DAMN YOU! SHUT UP!

HARLOW: (*Putting hand over mouth*) Ho hum.(*Stretches*)
Ho hum. Ho hum. Ho . . . Ho . . . HOoooooooooooo . . .
Ho hum.
(*Looking directly at KID*) Sit down you dumb
fuck!

(*THE KID sits down again, hands on his knees,
staring at HARLOW. Long pause.*)

THE KID: (*Serious/concentrated*) We can do anything we
want to do here . . . There's nobody around to watch.

HARLOW: (*Stretching languorously*) Just like grown-ups,
huh?

THE KID: (*Leaning towards her*) There's no one to watch.

HARLOW: (*Stretching more luxuriously*) No one can
see us, huh?

THE KID: That's right.

HARLOW: What do you want to do?

THE KID: Just what I said.

HARLOW: That's what you want ME to do.

THE KID: That's right!

HARLOW: Sit on a tack!

THE KID: You know that's what you'd like to do . . .

23

HARLOW: Sit on your lap and play with your cock?

THE KID: Yeah!

HARLOW: (*Stretching*) OOOOOoooooooh . . .(*Stretching arms*) Ho . . . Ho . . . Ho humm. You're out of your nut!

THE KID: There's nobody here, Baby!

HARLOW: So what!
Let me sleep. (*Curls up*)

(*Pause. HARLOW feigns sleep*)

THE KID: I don't want to pry any secrets from you.

HARLOW: I was just talking . . . That's all right.

THE KID: I really don't.

HARLOW: (*Sleepily*) It's all right.

THE KID: What shall we do?

HARLOW: Sleep.

THE KID: No! WE'RE ABSOLUTELY FREE!

HARLOW: (*Sleepily*) Shut up!

THE KID: This is perfect liberty! (*Pause*) We're divine!

HARLOW: Sure . . . Sure . . .

THE KID: Listen . . .

HARLOW: You're out of your nut!

THE KID: We're DIVINE!

HARLOW: Sure . . . Sure . . .
I've always known it. (*Feigning sleep*)

THE KID: You're not asleep.

HARLOW: Sure I am. I talk in my sleep!

THE KID: I know you're a real blond.

HARLOW: I know you're crazy and full of shit.
Let me sleep!

THE KID: You're great! There's only one you.

HARLOW: Sure . . . But I'm asleep.

THE KID: I like you asleep!

HARLOW: God damn you, shut up!

THE KID: I'll take off your shoes . . . (*Starting to kneel*)

HARLOW: (*Sitting up*) Keep away from my feet! (*Shaking head*) You are a creepy bastard aren't you!

THE KID: We're DIVINE!

HARLOW: Oh yeah! Yeah . . . Yeah . . .

THE KID: YOU'RE A REAL BLOND!

HARLOW: Sure.

THE KID: We're divine. We're in eternity!

HARLOW: Sure.

THE KID: I'm not trying to pry secrets from you.

HARLOW: I read that someplace.

THE KID: What?

HARLOW: That thing.

THE KID: Where.

HARLOW: Where what?

THE KID: Where did you read it?

HARLOW: In a comic book.

THE KID: (*Angrily*) Yeah!
Where did you read it?

HARLOW: IN A COMIC BOOK!

THE KID: OH YEAH!

HARLOW: O.K., maybe I didn't.

　　　Before you can pry any secrets from me you must first . . .

THE KID: Shut up!

HARLOW: All right!

THE KID: Listen, WE'RE DIVINE!

HARLOW: Sure! Divinity is blue velvet!

THE KID: And blond hair.

HARLOW: And buck teeth!

THE KID: —Where did you read it?

HARLOW: I made it up!

THE KID: Oh yeah! Where did you read it?

HARLOW: I made it up!

THE KID: Sure!

HARLOW: I THOUGHT OF IT!

THE KID: Oh yeah!

HARLOW: You bet your ass I did! —Or maybe I read it.

THE KID: I'll bet you got fat laying on your ass reading

comic books.

HARLOW: And eating chocolate goodies.

THE KID: Fuck you!

HARLOW: FUCK YOU!
        You call *me* fat — you dumb, creepy, buck
toothed bastard!

THE KID: Maybe that's divine! —Buck teeth, dumb,
creepy.

MARLOW: Maybe *divine* is nothing but blue velvet!

THE KID: What comic book?

HARLOW: It wasn't in a magazine! —Go to Hell!

THE KID: Say it again!

HARLOW: My God! My God!

THE KID: SAY IT AGAIN!

HARLOW: Ohh!

THE KID: Again!

HARLOW: OHH!

THE KID: Again!

HARLOW: Before you can pry any secrets . . .

THE KID: You're not fat!

HARLOW: Oh YEAH!

THE KID: Listen, WE'RE DIVINE!

HARLOW: I wouldn't listen to you shit in a rainbarrel!

THE KID: We're divine, Baby, we're DIVINE!
This is really it. We're really here!

HARLOW: Sure.

THE KID: I mean it!

HARLOW: Sure you mean it! You're crazier than fuck!

THE KID: Oh yeah! Come here and sit on my lap and lick
my boots!

HARLOW: You're full of it! You aren't even a man. You
wish you were a chick!

THE KID: Come here and sit on my lap. —And lick my
boots.

HARLOW: Why should I lick your boots?

THE KID: You'd love to!

HARLOW: You'd like to grab my blond hair in your hands!

THE KID: So what!

HARLOW: You'd like to see me crawl?

THE KID: (*Shrugs*)

HARLOW: Why should I lick your boots?

THE KID: Come here and sit on my lap.

HARLOW: Why do you want me to lick your boots?

THE KID: Because we're divine, Babe, divine, and there's nobody here!

HARLOW: Nobody to watch, huh?

THE KID: That's right.

HARLOW: What if I DID?

THE KID: Then you could touch my cock.

HARLOW: Just like grown-ups, huh?
You're full of shit!

THE KID: We're divine!

HARLOW: Sure!

THE KID: I'm divine.

HARLOW: And I suppose you think I'm not!

THE KID: Yeah. Come and sit on my lap and I'll give you a shot . . .

HARLOW: Not with that rod of yours — you'll make me laugh!

THE KID: And you can lick my boots!

HARLOW: What makes you think I want to sit on your lap or lick your boots?

THE KID: There's nobody here!

HARLOW: You mean people want to do it because there's nobody around?

THE KID: Sure!

HARLOW: What's so great about your boots?

THE KID: Rainbows reflected on sheer black!

HARLOW: O. k., what if I sit on your lap?

THE KID: And touch my cock?

HARLOW: My God!

THE KID: My bare cock with your hand!

HARLOW: I'm going to go to sleep!

THE KID: God damn you!

HARLOW: You've got a dirty mouth!
(*Pause*)
What did you mean when you said I'm an illusion?

THE KID: I didn't say it — you did. I said you're a bag of meat!

HARLOW: Then what's so great about me? —What do you want with a bag of meat? (Before you can pry any secrets from me, you must first find the real me! Which one will you pursue?)
What do you mean — bag of meat?

THE KID: Why don't you find the real you and pursue it yourself!

HARLOW: Screw you!

THE KID: Come over here and sit on my lap!

HARLOW: All right there's nobody here. So what!
(*Pause. No action. HARLOW curls herself up.*)
I'm going to sleep.

THE KID: A bag of meat is a bag of meat!

HARLOW: (*Sits bolt upright.*)

THE KID: Stuffed with fat and bones!

HARLOW: You're a pain in the ass!

THE KID: In eternity?

HARLOW: Sure, wherever you are!

THE KID: Good night!

HARLOW: Fuck you!
You're a prim little cunt for a tough guy!

THE KID: A bag of meat is a bag of meat!

HARLOW: (*Pulls dress up leg*) Look at that!

THE KID: Come and sit on my lap!

HARLOW: For Christ sake!

THE KID: What makes you think I want to pry secrets from you?

HARLOW: You don't interest me!

THE KID: Not in eternity?

HARLOW: Not even in eternity!

THE KID: I'll bet!

HARLOW: That's right!

THE KID: You're lying.

(*Pause. HARLOW feigns sleep.*)

33

Hey!
You're a NICE bag of meat!

HARLOW: For Christ sake!

THE KID: I like your leg.

HARLOW: It's a bag of meat.

THE KID: Yeah.

HARLOW: So?

THE KID: I like a nice bag of meat.

HARLOW: You're a crude S.O.B.

THE KID: And buck-toothed?

HARLOW: With your hair hanging half way down to your crack like a floozie!

THE KID: Before you can pry any secrets from me, you must first find the real me! Which one will you pursue?

HARLOW: Shit!

THE KID: Before you can pry any . . .

HARLOW: Shit!

THE KID: Before you can pry any secrets from me, you

must first find the real me . . .

HARLOW: O.k., who are you?

THE KID: Blue velvet.

HARLOW: That's an illusion. You look like a hunk of meat.

THE KID: Sit on my lap!

HARLOW: And I suppose I'm supposed to be blond hair— like blond hair on blue velvet?

THE KID: Suit yourself!

HARLOW: O.k., together we're blond hair on blue velvet.

THE KID: That's not enough.

HARLOW: What's not enough?

THE KID: Blond hair on blue velvet!

HARLOW: I suppose because there's nobody around there should be something more?

THE KID: Yeah!

HARLOW: Like what?

THE KID: Like . . .

HARLOW: —Sit on a tack!

THE KID: It's not a tack you'd like to sit on.

HARLOW: Yeah!

THE KID: It's something else.

HARLOW: Like what? Your lap?

THE KID: You're close!

HARLOW: Awhh!
(*Pause*)

THE KID: Blond hair on blue velvet isn't enough!
Maybe I love you.

HARLOW: What's love!
You're jealous of my beauty!

THE KID: I don't give a fuck about your beauty! If I
wanted you I'd want YOU!

HARLOW: Oh yeah?
I'm sick of hearing about your boots!

THE KID: When I say *boots* I don't mean boots.

HARLOW: What do you mean then?

THE KID: When I say blond hair and blue velvet I don't
mean that either.

HARLOW: What do you mean then?

THE KID: By boots?

HARLOW: Yeah, by boots.

THE KID: I don't give a fuck about beauty! If I wanted you I'd want YOU!

HARLOW: You said that. What do you mean by boots?

THE KID: My cock!

HARLOW: Oh my God!

THE KID: MY COCK!

HARLOW: I'm going to look at the walls. (*HARLOW walks stroking walls*)
    They're nice!

THE KID: I'm your walls!

HARLOW: Shit! (*Pause*)
    What do you mean I'm fat?

THE KID: I said you're a real blond!
    (*Pause*)
    I'm your walls to rub against.

HARLOW: HERE?

THE KID: Anywhere!

HARLOW: They're soft.

THE KID: I'm soft too.
And hard as a rock!

HARLOW: (*Walks looking at walls and stroking them.
Looks directly at KID*)
Bull shit!
Before you can pry any secrets from me, you
must first find the real me!

THE KID: Yeah!

HARLOW: Find it!

THE KID: Sit on my lap and stroke my cock!

HARLOW: You're a fucking monomaniac!

THE KID: And lick my boots.

HARLOW: You said it wasn't your boots!
. . . Never mind!

THE KID: Sit on my lap . . .

HARLOW: And touch your cock?

THE KID: There's nobody here!

HARLOW: Just like grown-ups, huh?
Why isn't blond hair on blue velvet enough.

THE KID: Because you're a bag of meat!

HARLOW: I'm an illusion.
What do you mean you'd want ME?
Why isn't blond hair on blue velvet enough?

THE KID: Because you're a bag of meat!

HARLOW: I'm a real BLOND!

THE KID: That's what I said.

HARLOW: You wanted to see my baby pictures.

THE KID: I believed it!

HARLOW: Why do you want ME?

THE KID: Because you're here!

HARLOW: Fuck you!

THE KID: That's the price you pay!

HARLOW: What? What price?

THE KID: The price for being here.

HARLOW: Piss!

THE KID: Piss on you!

HARLOW: You ARE JEALOUS of my beauty!

THE KID: We're DIVINE, Babe, divine!

HARLOW: Well, what the Hell does that mean?

THE KID: We're DIVINE, Babe, divine!

HARLOW: Well, what the Hell does that mean?

THE KID: We're HERE!

HARLOW: If being HERE is divine it's a bunch of shit! Maybe I don't even like it here . . . looking at your crazy eyes, and buck teeth and long hair! And hearing all of that crap about blond hair and blue velvet! Besides you're an ugly fucker! You aren't even my type!

THE KID: You wouldn't know divine from a handful of shit. You're here by accident!

HARLOW: If you're divine it's a big mistake!
If you're divine I'd rather be elsewhere!

THE KID: Lying on a bed with a magazine?

HARLOW: Yeah.

THE KID: You'd be divine there too.

HARLOW: You said I wouldn't know divine from a hand-ful of shit!

THE KID: You wouldn't know it but you'd be there!

HARLOW: WHERE?

THE KID: Here!

HARLOW: Where's here?

THE KID: Where we're divine!

HARLOW: I wouldn't be divine with you on a bet! You're full of shit and you're a God damn monomaniac bore!

THE KID: What about my cock?

HARLOW: Ohhh!

THE KID: I can't help that I'm divine. I didn't plan it. I'm HERE! —I *decided* it.

HARLOW: Decided what?

THE KID: I decided it — but I didn't plan it!

HARLOW: Decided what?

THE KID: To be HERE — to be divine!

HARLOW: ... CRAP! What do you mean *I'm* here by accident? I thought it out every step of the way.

THE KID: Then you wanted to be with me!

HARLOW: You're full of it — and I'm sick of hearing you. —I *planned* it!

41

THE KID: Planned what?

HARLOW: Being here. Being divine. Being wherever I am with blond hair!

THE KID: Then you wanted to be with ME!
I decided it — and it happened.

HARLOW: Then you wanted to be with *me*!

THE KID: I never even heard of you!

HARLOW: How did you make it happen?

THE KID: By deciding it — deciding to be divine.

HARLOW: And we're here together.

THE KID: That's right!

HARLOW: Before you can pry any secrets from me, you must first find the real me! Which one will you pursue?

THE KID: You're a nice bag of meat!

HARLOW: For Christ sake!

THE KID: I like your leg.

HARLOW: It's a bag of meat.

THE KID: Yeah.

HARLOW: So?

THE KID: I like a nice bag of meat.

HARLOW: And we're divine!

THE KID: And we're free, this is liberty, and there's no-body here!

HARLOW: It's always that way.

THE KID: That's what I mean!

HARLOW: O.k., this is liberty, we're free, and there's no-body here . . . So . . . ?

THE KID: Sit on my lap and touch my cock.

HARLOW: And what about your boots?

THE KID: Forget that. I'll kneel and kiss your feet.

HARLOW: You already tried that.

THE KID: Yes.
I'll do it again. (*Starting to kneel*)

HARLOW: (*Pulling feet back*) The fuck you will!
(*Pause*) You know, you look like you're blind.
Or maybe crazy, or angry. You're out of your mind. No, not blind . . . something else . . .

THE KID: I'm seeing everywhere.

43

HARLOW: Yeah?

THE KID: You are too.

HARLOW: O.k., we're seeing everywhere in liberty, huh?

THE KID: Sure.
I'll take off your shoes!

HARLOW: Get away! I'm here because I planned it and I'll do what I please.

THE KID: I'm not raping you.

HARLOW: Yeah?
(*Pause*)
What do you mean you're here because you decided?

THE KID: I decided to be divine — and you're divine too.

HARLOW: So what! I didn't ask for you!

THE KID: Nor did I ask for you — but we're blond hair on blue velvet.

HARLOW: You said that wasn't it — blond hair on blue velvet isn't it!

THE KID: It's not. It's something more.

HARLOW: Like?

THE KID: Like being a bag of meat and being divine in liberty.

HARLOW: (*Angrily*) With your hair down to your crack!

THE KID: Sure. Sit on my lap and I'll show you how.

HARLOW: How what?

THE KID: How to be divine!

HARLOW: I'm so divine I'm free of you and all your shit.

THE KID: Nobody's free of being divine!

HARLOW: O.K., I'M SICK OF ALL THIS SHIT AND I'M TIRED OF HEARING YOU RAVE ABOUT *DIVINE* AND *LIBERTY!* You tricked me into talking with you.

THE KID: YOU DON'T HAVE ANY CHOICE — you're here, and you're divine and free, and you're going to sit on my lap and touch my cock. You're going to listen because you're free, and you're going to do what I tell you! And we're going to do a lot more too. And if you don't (then) I'm going to do it all to you. AND YOU'RE GOING TO TAKE ALL THAT SHIT ABOUT ME BEING A CUNT AND YOU'RE GOING TO SWALLOW IT UP YOUR DIRTY ASS AGAIN!

HARLOW: LISTEN, YOU LITTLE FUCKER, YOU MAY RAPE ME BUT . . .

THE KID: I WOULDN'T TOUCH YOU!

HARLOW: You wouldn't, huh?

THE KID: Not till you ask.

HARLOW: I'll never ask!

THE KID: Not till you're willing!

HARLOW: You just threatened me with rape!

THE KID: Yeah! But I wouldn't touch you with a long stick!

HARLOW: (*Taking deep breath*) O.k., what's *divine*?

THE KID: *Divine* is *free*!

HARLOW: And there's nobody here? AND WE'RE BAGS OF MEAT?

THE KID: You're a bag of meat!

HARLOW: And what are you?

THE KID: I am too — and something more!

HARLOW: Like what?
—You wouldn't dare touch me!

THE KID: I'd dare — but I wouldn't!

HARLOW: YOU'RE SCARED!

THE KID: Hmm!
> (*KID grabs HARLOW and wrestles with her.*)

HARLOW: GODDAMN YOU! LET LOOSE OF ME
YOU DIRTY FUCKER!
> GOD DAMN YOU! OH! OH! GOD DAMN
YOU!!

> (*THE KID gets HARLOW'S shoes off and bites
her foot. HARLOW screams.*)
> (*Gritting teeth*) Oh, you dirty fucker! You
dirty God damn son of a bitch. . . . I think it's bleeding.
(*She holds up foot to look at it closely.*)

THE KID: (*Turns his back on HARLOW. Goes and looks
at the velvet walls.*)

HARLOW: YOU TORE MY STOCKING! YOU TORE
MY STOCKING WITH YOUR TEETH! YOU TORE
MY STOCKING WITH YOUR ROTTEN TEETH!

THE KID: (*Sneeringly*) Yeah, that's *divine*!

HARLOW: (*Nursing her foot*) Now you are being a cunt
—with that silly sneer.
> Oh, my poor foot!
> You are a crazy bastard! Biting a woman's foot!
Look what you did to my stocking! —I think there's
some blood! Oh, my God, there's going to be blood!

THE KID: Quit squeezing it.

HARLOW: I'm going to be sick.

47

THE KID: The Hell you are!

HARLOW: Blood makes me sick.

THE KID: Baloney!
Quit squeezing it!

HARLOW: Look at my stocking! Look at that tear!

THE KID: Take your stockings off!

HARLOW: (*Squintingly*) No telling where you'd bite me then.

THE KID: Come here and sit on my lap.

HARLOW: You crazy, crazy bastard — I don't know why we have to be HERE!
(*Squeezing*) Oh, my God, there's blood!

THE KID: Let me see!

HARLOW: What are you a fucking vampire. Get away from me! Get away you son of a bitch! Get away from me or I'll . . .

THE KID: Scream?

HARLOW: I wouldn't scream — I can take care of you.

THE KID: Why wouldn't you scream? —Because you want to be *here*?

HARLOW: (*Squeezing*) Fuck you! —Look there's some blood!

THE KID: Where?

HARLOW: Right by the toe. (*Pointing*)

THE KID: Do you like it?

HARLOW: Are you kidding?

THE KID: You squeezed it.

HARLOW: My God, I can't stand blood.

THE KID: You feel faint?

HARLOW: You sadist!

THE KID: Sit on my lap!

HARLOW: You're crazier than a hoot owl. You threw me down and bit my foot like some fucking Jack the Ripper maniac!

THE KID: You liked it.

HARLOW: You're full of shit! (*Studies toe*) Look at that! You like the blood. There, take a good look at it! (*Stretching tear with her finger*) Look at that! — Where's my comb? (*Combs hair*)

THE KID: I like your breasts too.

49

HARLOW: (*Sneeringly*) It's about time you noticed them. That makes me very happy! I suppose you'd like to draw blood out of them too! I suppose you'd like to bite the nipples off — you sadist pervert!

THE KID: You asked me to.

HARLOW: To what — bite my tits off?

THE KID: To put you in your place.

HARLOW: I suppose biting a woman on the foot puts her in her place? You make me laugh!
Look at that ruined stocking you fucking creep!

THE KID: It looks good! I'm beginning to want you.

HARLOW: Isn't that romantic! (*Taking mirror*) Get out of the light!

THE KID: What do you see?

HARLOW: If you'd get out of the light I'd see something besides your fucking shadow!

THE KID: I like your breasts.

HARLOW: So does everybody! (*Pause*) Is everybody divine?

THE KID: Before you can pry any secrets from me, you must first find the real me!

HARLOW: Fuck off! (*Combing hair again*)
(*Angrily*) Look at that stocking!
(*Pause. Thoughtful*)
Do you think everybody is divine?

THE KID: How should I know?

HARLOW: What do you *think*?

THE KID: Sure!

HARLOW: I don't!

THE KID: Don't what?

HARLOW: Think they're divine!

THE KID: Yeah?

HARLOW: STAY A GOOD LONG DISTANCE AWAY
FROM ME!

THE KID: Why not?

HARLOW: Maybe they are . . .

THE KID: Are what?

HARLOW: Divine. Maybe they're divine and don't
know it!

THE KID: That's what I'm trying to tell *you*.

HARLOW: Yeah, by biting my poor foot till it bleeds . . .

THE KID: You squeezed it till it bled.

HARLOW: And ruining my stocking!

THE KID: You called me a cunt!

HARLOW: Yeah? Maybe I'm sorry.
(*Pause*)
And maybe I'm not!

THE KID: Take off your stockings!

HARLOW: —Maybe you'd like to see my tits too?

THE KID: Sure.

HARLOW: You make me laugh!

THE KID: Take off your stockings.

HARLOW: You'd probably lick the blood right off my toe.

THE KID: Maybe I would if I could find it.

HARLOW: What do you mean, if you could find it! IT'S
THERE! Right there! Look! (*Puts her leg up on the chair*)
There it is right by my toe! Right on the fucking stocking
you've ruined!

THE KID: (*Puts his hand on her thigh*)

52

HARLOW: GET YOUR HAND OFF, YOU CRUMBY
BASTARD!
　　　　　If you ever touch me I'll kill you — you . . .

THE KID: Cunt?

HARLOW: You filthy sadist . . . (*Struggling for words*)

THE KID: Listen, Baby, we're divine . . .

HARLOW: FOR CHRIST SAKE!
　　　　　—Look at that stocking— it's wiped out!

THE KID: Take it off then. Be divine!

HARLOW: Who's afraid to be divine! If taking off my
stocking is divine then you're a creep!

THE KID: It's divine to you — not to me!

HARLOW: You're the one who'll get the kick!

THE KID: It'll be your act!

HARLOW: Whataya mean my *act*?

THE KID: Your DEED!

HARLOW: Taking off my stocking will be my divine
deed?

THE KID: Yeah!

53

HARLOW: O.k.! (*Takes off stocking. Holds it up.*)
  LOOK AT THAT!

THE KID: I'm watching you be divine.

HARLOW: SHIT!
          —I could put my arm through that tear!

THE KID: You stretched it. Picking and tearing for blood.

HARLOW: YOU RUINED MY STOCKING!

THE KID: Yeah. So?

HARLOW: You ugly rat!

THE KID: HUH! (*Indifferently*)

HARLOW: I suppose it doesn't matter because we're
  divine!

THE KID: That's right!

HARLOW: What's a stocking in eternity, huh?

THE KID: Yeah, what's a stocking in eternity, huh?
  (*Mocking*)

HARLOW: (*Nursing foot*) And what's a toe?

THE KID: That's right.

HARLOW: Well, it's my toe! What if I bit yours?

THE KID: Go ahead! (*Smiles*)

HARLOW: You silly shit!

THE KID: I can be crazy and divine, or silly and divine—
or violent and divine!

HARLOW: *I could too!*

THE KID: Then why don't you?

HARLOW: Look at that toe. The stocking is completely
ruined . . .
                  How?

THE KID: Sit on my lap and . . .

HARLOW: SHUT . . .

THE KID: You're divine!!

HARLOW: UP!

THE KID: Stop!

HARLOW: (*Cynically*) All right. (*Standing one foot on
chair holding stocking up*)

THE KID: One bare leg — in a pale dress — you're holding an empty stocking up — your blond hair is a crown,
it's an emblem of eternity — there's blood on your bare
foot — your hair is mussed, there's anger in your eyes
and you're aroused!

HARLOW: You're fucking right I am!

THE KID: SHUT UP!
One bare leg — in a pale dress — you're holding an empty stocking up — it hangs in the light . . .

HARLOW: ISN'T THAT POETIC!

THE KID: Moist from your thighs . . .

HARLOW: From wrestling with you, you dumb fuck!

THE KID: YOU'RE REAL NOW!

HARLOW: OF COURSE I AM — THAT SLOBBER
DOESN'T MAKE ME MORE REAL!

THE KID: BUT BITING DID!

HARLOW: FUCK YOU!

THE KID: Take the other one off!

HARLOW: Shit.

THE KID: Take it off!

HARLOW: Maybe I will. I look like a fool with one stocking on and one off. (*She begins to take it off*)

THE KID: There's nobody here to watch.

HARLOW: Nobody to see me be a fool, huh? (*Pauses with*
56

stocking)
>I thought you wanted me to take it off.
>What do you mean biting my foot made me real?

THE KID: It makes me real — not you.

HARLOW: We're both real — skip it. (*Taking stocking off*)

THE KID: Which one of you will I pursue.

HARLOW: Fuck off!

THE KID: Which one?

HARLOW: There's only one me!

THE KID: What?

HARLOW: One me! There's only one ME!

THE KID: Bull shit!

HARLOW: Whataya mean?

THE KID: You convinced me otherwise.

HARLOW: Otherwise than what?

THE KID: That there's more than one you!

HARLOW: Jesus, that toe still hurts!

THE KID: Which one is divine?

HARLOW: Look at that tooth mark!

THE KID: Yeah.
             Which one is divine?

HARLOW: I'M DIVINE!

THE KID: Sure, I've heard that before.

HARLOW: I'm divine you son of a bitch — and you're divine too!

THE KID: Yeah!

HARLOW: And you're after my beauty!

THE KID: What beauty?

HARLOW: My blond beauty!

THE KID: I'm only after *my* beauty!

HARLOW: You're a weird fuck!

THE KID: We're in Heaven.

HARLOW: It's a heaven full of tooth marks then!

THE KID: This IS HEAVEN!

HARLOW: You're only after my beauty!

THE KID: Take off your pants!

HARLOW: WHAT!

THE KID: Take off your pants!

HARLOW: Maybe I will! Maybe I just will to see what you do. (*Harlow takes off her pants.*)

THE KID: Hand them to me.

HARLOW: You're crazy!

THE KID: Hand them to me.

HARLOW: You're out of your nut!

(*THE KID takes the panties from HARLOW who stands staring at him*)

HARLOW: Give them back you fucker!

THE KID: They're warm.

HARLOW: What did you expect — ice?

THE KID: And they're moist.

HARLOW: You expect sand? Now give them back!

THE KID: (*He tears them in half*)

HARLOW: (*Gasping with astonishment*) YOU'RE CRAZY!

(*Picking up the pieces*) My poor panties. My God, My God.

THE KID: Sit on my lap!

HARLOW: YOU'RE A FUCKING MANIAC! You're a raving drooling MURDERER!

THE KID: We're divine and we're flesh and blood and anything else is shit! IF WE DON'T DO WHAT WE WANT WE'RE NOT DIVINE! WHAT DO YOU WANT?

HARLOW: I don't know!

THE KID: What do you want?

HARLOW: My God, my clothes! Oh, my poor clothes!

THE KID: What do you want?

HARLOW: SHUT UP! SHUT UP! LOOK AT THESE FUCKING RAGS! YOU'VE BITTEN ME AND TORN UP MY CLOTHES! WHAT IN THE HELL IS HAPPEN-ING. Where are we? Who the Hell are you? Who am I? Look at my fucking clothes . . . my clothes . . . And my God damn hair! Where's my comb?
— Why did you do that?

THE KID: I wanted to.

HARLOW: (*Shaking head and backing away*) You're vio-lent — and you're crazy!

THE KID: You don't need clothes in eternity except for decoration. —A toothmark goes away in Heaven or Hell. You don't need anything to perpetuate illusion. I Don't want your beauty or any other — I want only to enact mine.

HARLOW: YOU'RE ALMOST BEAUTIFUL!

THE KID: Yeah.

HARLOW: You're too fucking dumb to talk but you're almost beautiful.

THE KID: It's like a vision . . .

HARLOW: That's a dumb word.

THE KID: What?

HARLOW: Vision — vision is a dumb word.

THE KID: What if I said you're as beautiful as a vision!

HARLOW: It sounds better then.

THE KID: Sit on my lap.

HARLOW: YOU'RE OUT OF YOUR MIND! Before you can pry any secrets out of me you must first find the real me!

THE KID: I already have!

HARLOW: Where?

THE KID: THERE! (*Points to panties on the floor*)

HARLOW: You're full of shit THAT'S NOT ME! That's a pair of torn panties!

THE KID: What's you then?

HARLOW: ME . . . HERE . . . ME . . .

THE KID: A BAG OF MEAT!

HARLOW: YEAH! A BAG OF MEAT!

THE KID: Swirling in eternity?

HARLOW: Yeah, swirling in eternity! Or solid HERE — it doesn't make any difference!

THE KID: Is that what you want?

HARLOW: Yeah!

THE KID: Are you sure?

HARLOW: I planned it!

THE KID: What did you plan?

HARLOW: To be in eternity!

THE KID: How did you plan it.

HARLOW: By doing what I want!

THE KID: That's called destiny!

HARLOW: To do what you want?

THE KID: Yeah!

HARLOW: I guess you said it!
        What it is . . . Destiny.
        — I DON'T WANT TO TALK TO YOU! YOU
TORE UP MY PANTIES!

THE KID: In eternity?

HARLOW: Yeah, you tore up my panties in eternity! Or
any other fucking place. You tore up my pants!

THE KID: And you called me a cunt!

HARLOW: Yeah, I called you a cunt!

THE KID: In eternity!

HARLOW: Yeah, I called you a cunt in eternity!

THE KID: Come here and sit on my lap.

HARLOW: You're out of your mind!

THE KID: What do you want?

HARLOW: I want to stand here and comb my hair —

while I figure what to do about you.

THE KID: What do you want to do?

HARLOW: Will you shut up! — I'm combing my hair!

THE KID: You're combing your blond hair in eternity and you don't know what to do there!

HARLOW: Yeah!

THE KID: And you planned to be there?

HARLOW: Where?

THE KID: Here.

HARLOW: Yeah!
            —And you decided to be here?

THE KID: Yeah.

HARLOW: How did you decide?

THE KID: By doing what I wanted to do.

HARLOW: And that's called destiny?

THE KID: Yeah, it's only a word. People call destiny doing what you want to do.

HARLOW: What the bag of meat tells you to do?

THE KID: Yeah.

HARLOW: What does your bag of meat tell you to do?

THE KID: To get you on my lap.

HARLOW: And that's why you tore up my panties and bit my toe?

THE KID: — I did what I wanted to do.

HARLOW: What if that was what I want you to do?

THE KID: It's the same thing — it doesn't matter.

HARLOW: WHY NOT?

THE KID: We want the same thing and (we) enact it between us.

HARLOW: BULLSHIT!

THE KID: What?

HARLOW: Just bullshit!
—What do you mean 'between us'?

THE KID: RIGHT HERE!

HARLOW: You're full of it. Get out of the light — I'm combing my hair.
O.k., what's destiny? (*Combing her hair.*)

THE KID: It's doing what you want to do. Destiny is only a word but it's turned into a religion. Then it's laughed at.

HARLOW: Why not?

THE KID: It should be.

HARLOW: WHAT MATTERS?

THE KID: We're here!

HARLOW: Keep the fuck away from me!

THE KID: I'm not even near.

HARLOW: Before you can pry any secrets from me, you must first find the real me! Which one will you pursue?

THE KID: You're right here!
  —Sit on my lap . . .

HARLOW: And touch your thing?

THE KID: There's nobody here!

HARLOW: Just like grown-ups, huh?
  Why isn't blond hair on blue velvet enough?

THE KID: Because you're a bag of meat!

HARLOW: What do you mean you'd want ME?
  Why isn't blond hair on blue velvet enough?
  I'm a real blond.

THE KID: That's what I said!

HARLOW: (*Combing hair*) You tore my panties up!

THE KID: That's what I wanted.

HARLOW: You're full of shit! If destiny is to tear a girl's panties up — then you're full of it!
  Look at those poor rags.

THE KID: Yeah.

HARLOW: Look at 'em!

THE KID: Sure.

HARLOW: You tore my panties up!

THE KID: Yeah!

HARLOW: You tore them in half — and bit me on the toe — and threw me on the floor — and ruined my stocking!

THE KID: You ruined your stocking.

HARLOW: You bit my fucking toe! AND TORE MY PANTIES UP!

THE KID: That's what you wanted!

HARLOW: BULL SHIT!

THE KID: That's what you said!

Before you can pry any secrets out of me, you
must first find the real me! Which one will you pursue?

HARLOW: Fuck off! (*Combs hair energetically*)
That's a shitty destiny!

THE KID: It's only a step.

HARLOW: How can it be a step without being destiny?

THE KID: Who knows?

HARLOW: Yeah ?

THE KID: Yeah.

HARLOW: You fucking rat! — I'm disheveled.

THE KID: Good.

HARLOW: I'm disheveled!

THE KID: In eternity.
—You look good!

HARLOW: Yeah, I'm disheveled in eternity — and that's
destiny . . .

THE KID: It doesn't matter! You're here and you look
good!

HARLOW: Where?

THE KID: HERE! —And you look good!

HARLOW: You said that and I'm tired of hearing it!

THE KID: YOU LOOK GOOD!

HARLOW: In eternity?

THE KID: Yeah!

HARLOW: Well, I don't like it!
— You're DUMB!

THE KID: It doesn't matter!

HARLOW: I'm sick of hearing you say it doesn't matter!

THE KID: So what! We're here. It doesn't matter whether
it matters — there's nobody around to watch!

HARLOW: You're almost beautiful — you're so fucking
dumb.

THE KID: It doesn't matter!

HARLOW: Awh shit!
There's nothing here but blond hair and blue
velvet.

THE KID: And a lot more.

HARLOW: MORE WHAT?

THE KID: It hasn't happened. — Sit on my lap.

HARLOW: *And lick your boots?*

THE KID: (No,) skip that.

HARLOW: Skip it, huh?

THE KID: Yeah, skip it. Sit on my lap.

HARLOW: You're a maniac! What if I don't? What'll you
do — tear my dress up? —Or kick my head?

THE KID: I might.

HARLOW: You might, huh?
YOU WOULDN'T DARE!

THE KID: That's what you said before.

HARLOW: O.k., I said it before.

THE KID: What?

HARLOW: Whatever I said. —Whatever I said, I said
before.

THE KID: That's right. (yeah)

HARLOW: You monomaniac! You're so fucking dumb
you make me puke! You're so screwed up you might do
anything.

THE KID: That's right.

HARLOW: YOU'RE DUMB!

THE KID: You're beautiful!

HARLOW: YOU'RE DUMB! DUMB! DUMB!

THE KID: Does it matter?

HARLOW: (*Pause*) I DON'T KNOW.

THE KID: Don't know what?

HARLOW: Does it matter?

THE KID: Yeah.

HARLOW: You said nothing MATTERS!

THE KID: It matters to ME.
(*Pause*)

HARLOW: Why don't you want me to lick your boots?

THE KID: I changed my mind!

HARLOW: In eternity?

THE KID: Sit on my lap.

HARLOW: And lick your boots?

THE KID: We're divine and we're flesh and blood and anything else is shit! IF WE DON'T DO WHAT WE WANT — WE'RE NOT DIVINE! What do you want?

HARLOW: I don't know.
 —You dumb cunt!
 (*Looking*) Where are my shoes?

THE KID: I'll put them on your feet.

HARLOW: The fuck you will!
 Get out of my way.

THE KID: Where would you go?

HARLOW: I'll stay right here.

THE KID: In eternity?

HARLOW: Yeah. (*Finds shoes*)

THE KID: Is that what you want?

HARLOW: Yeah, I'm going to stay right here!

THE KID: There's nobody here to watch!

HARLOW: (*Starts to put on shoe*)

THE KID: Don't put them on!

HARLOW: Why not!

THE KID: We're divine, Babe, divine!

HARLOW: Maybe I won't — I like the look on your face.
I like to see you be a cunt! (*Stretches her legs out — arching her feet*)

THE KID: What do you want?

HARLOW: (*Mocking*) Well, what do you want? —Or
maybe I shouldn't ask — I already know!

THE KID: How do you know?

HARLOW: I heard what you said. You said it over and
over till it makes me puke!
—Where's my comb?

THE KID: Look yourself!
It's on the table under your shoes.

HARLOW: I know that — I just like to hear you talk!

THE KID: Yeah!
What do you want?

HARLOW: What if I said — 'whatever you want'?

THE KID: You're full of shit!

HARLOW: GOD DAMN YOU, I'M SICK OF THIS!

THE KID: Shut up, and sit on my lap!

HARLOW: What does it matter if I do or don't?

THE KID: It matters in eternity!

HARLOW: Like being a bag of meat matters?

THE KID: Yeah.

HARLOW: What are we doing here?

THE KID: It matters but I don't give a shit!

HARLOW: You mean we're HERE!

THE KID: Yeah.

HARLOW: What'll we do?

THE KID: WHAT I WANT!

HARLOW: WHAT ABOUT ME?

THE KID: Whatever you want!

HARLOW: Yeah!
You're a dumb fuck!

THE KID: And you're a bag of meat!

HARLOW: And nothing more?

THE KID: Where we are — only the bag of meat matters.

HARLOW: Because there's nobody around to watch?

THE KID: Yeah.

HARLOW: And you tore my panties up.

THE KID: Yes.

HARLOW: And you bit me on the toe!

THE KID: Yeah.

HARLOW: And you threw me down on the floor!

THE KID: Yeah.

HARLOW: And you might do anything you want!

THE KID: Sure.

HARLOW: And what about me?

THE KID: That's up to you.

HARLOW: What if I sit on your lap?

THE KID: You called me a cunt!

HARLOW: YEAH, WITH YOUR HAIR HANGING DOWN TO YOUR ASS AND BUCK TEETH!

THE KID: What does it matter?

HARLOW: IT MATTERS PLENTY, YOU FUCKING
SHIT! (*In fury*) WHAT IF I SIT ON YOUR LAP!

THE KID: Try it and see!

HARLOW: I wouldn't touch you with a dirty stick!
(*Pause*)
What if I did sit on your lap?

THE KID: Try it and see.

HARLOW: DON'T GET NEAR ME!!

THE KID: I didn't move.

HARLOW: You're full of it, buddy!
Look at my pants! (*Holding them up*)

THE KID: So what!

HARLOW: Stay right where you are!

THE KID: Shut up! (*Not moving*)

HARLOW: What do you want?

THE KID: Whatever I say I want!

HARLOW: You said you wanted me to lick your boots!

THE KID: O.k., do what you want.

HARLOW: And now you don't.

THE KID: Sit on my lap!

HARLOW: WHAT IF I WALK OVER AND SIT ON
YOUR LAP?

THE KID: Yeah.

HARLOW: What if I do?

THE KID: Try it and see.

HARLOW: What would you do?

THE KID: How would I know?
—Can't you guess?

HARLOW: What do you want me to do?

THE KID: I already said.

HARLOW: Rub your joint?

THE KID: Yeah. That's a place to start.

HARLOW: (*Hurls panties at him*) THERE'S A START!

THE KID: —We're already HERE. We don't need a start.

HARLOW: Yeah, that's what YOU said!

THE KID: We've started.

HARLOW: Oh yeah! Fuck you!

THE KID: What do you want?

HARLOW: To look at the walls. (*She walks stroking the walls.*)

>	(*THE KID takes out handkerchief and polishes toes of his boots*)

HARLOW: WHAT IF I SAID YOU'RE NOT A CUNT?

THE KID: So what! (*Polishing*)

HARLOW: WHAT IF I SAID YOU'RE NOT A CUNT?

THE KID: So what!

HARLOW: I've got to use words!

THE KID: Oh yeah!

HARLOW: WHAT DO YOU WANT? What the goddam Hell do you want?

THE KID: I want whatever I want!

HARLOW: I've got to use words!

THE KID: Oh yeah!

HARLOW: I like you (*Suddenly*)
You're insane and violent but I like you!

THE KID: So what!

HARLOW: I've got to use words!

THE KID: Oh yeah!

HARLOW: What do you want.

THE KID: I want whatever I want!

HARLOW: Well?

THE KID: Whatever I want!

HARLOW: Well WHAT do you want?

THE KID: Maybe I want to be beautiful!

HARLOW: Awh! WHAT DO YOU WANT?

THE KID: Before you can pry any secrets from me, you
must first find the real me! Which one will you pursue?

HARLOW: What makes you think I want to pry secrets
from YOU?

THE KID: Because I'm so beautiful.

HARLOW: So what!

THE KID: You want to be as beautiful as I am.

HARLOW: Oh yeah!

THE KID: Before you can pry any secrets from me, you must first find the real me! Which one will you pursue?

HARLOW: (*Coming closer*) What makes you think I want to pry any secrets from you?

THE KID: Because I'm so beautiful.

HARLOW: So what!

THE KID: You want to be as beautiful as I am!

HARLOW: Oh yeah! (*Kneels quickly and grabs his boots*)
I'VE GOT YOU!
YOU'RE BEAUTIFUL!

THE KID: It's an illusion!

(*HARLOW hugs the boots and caresses them*)

HARLOW: There are rainbows on them — rainbows reflected on sheer black!

(*KID reaches over and takes HARLOW'S head*)

THE KID: Now I've got your blond hair in my hands.

HARLOW: There are rainbows on them — rainbows reflected on sheer black!

THE KID: Now I've got your blond hair in my hands!

HARLOW: There are rainbows on them — rainbows reflected on sheer black!

THE KID: Now I've got your blond hair in my hands.

HARLOW: (*Looking up at KID*) You've got my blond hair in your hands.
There's nobody around to watch!
You tore my panties up and you bit my toe!

THE KID: Yeah.

HARLOW: There's nobody around to watch.

THE KID: No, there's not.

HARLOW: What'll we do?

(*THE KID pulls HARLOW up into his lap*)

THE KID: (*Looking into HARLOW'S eyes*) — Now I've got your blond hair in my hands.

HARLOW: —And we're all alone!

(*HARLOW sitting on KID'S lap with one arm around his neck — he kisses her on the shoulder and neck —she strokes his cock . . .*)

HARLOW: My God, we're really here!

(*They begin to twist in the chair* — THE KID *slips gradually to the floor at HARLOW'S feet*)

HARLOW: —And we're all alone!

(*Kneeling, THE KID takes HARLOW'S foot in his hand and kisses it. He kisses the other foot. He presses his head against her thighs and holds it there. His hands clutch her bare feet behind his back. He lets loose of her feet pressing head more tightly against her thighs. She arches her back. He grasps her feet again burying his head in her thighs. He raises his head as if to speak and drops it to her thighs again. He lets loose of her feet and grasps them again. He lets loose of her feet and reaches up and moves her dress up her thighs. He clutches her feet behind him again. He grasps her thighs and presses his face between them, kissing her. HARLOW stiffens and arches her body . . .*)

HARLOW: (*Ecstatically*) STAR! STAR! STAR! OH MY GOD —! STAR! STAR! STAR! STAR! STAR! OH MY GOD —! STAR! STAR! YOU'RE NEXT! OH MY GOD —! BLUE-BLACK STAR! STAR! STAR! STAR! STAR! STAR! STAR! STAR! STAR! STAR! STAR! STAR! STAR! STAR! STAR! STAR! STAR!

(—curtain—)

AFTERWORD

AFTERWORD

The Beard was presented four times before direct police intervention. First by the Actor's Workshop of San Francisco, where it proved to be too much for that organization: despite the efforts of the director, the author and the actors, the Workshop establishment impeded in every possible way a performance of the play — including forbiding the presence of newspaper reviewers. Despite this censorship, Michael Grieg's review (heralding the play as the "most effectively upsetting and creatively stimulating work by a local writer that the workshop has ever presented") slipped into the San Francisco Chronicle. *The Beard* was next presented at the huge Rock and Roll *Fillmore Auditorium* to a wildly enthusiastic capacity crowd, where it was accompanied by Anthony Martin's light projections and a sound system utilizing rock music. The third and fourth performances of Michael McClure's *The Beard* took place at San Francisco's North Beach theater night club, *The Committee*. These two performances were surreptitiously tape recorded by the San Francisco Police Department, and at the fifth presentation, again at *The Committee*, police interrupted the ending of the play by filming it with whirring cameras, and then hurried backstage to arrest Mr. Bright (*Billy the Kid*) and Miss Dixon (*Harlow*). Alternately, the actors were charged with "obscenity," then "conspiracy to commit a felony" and finally with "lewd and dissolute conduct in a public place."

Twelve days later, *The Beard*, now represented by the American Civil Liberties Union (after an offer of help from Melvin Belli), was presented in Berkeley by *Rare Angel Pro-*

ductions to a capacity crowd, which included more than one hundred expert witnesses. These witnesses, invited by *Rare Angel Productions*, included Lawrence Ferlinghetti, Alan Watts, members of the academic community, members of the clergy, and photographers and tape-recording crews whose function was to record the police filming and taping of the performance. Seven members of the Berkeley Police and District Attorney's department arrived two hours before the performance, and began harassment of the actors, the author, and the stage crew. Malcom Burnstein of the ACLU and the author forbade any taping or filming of the performance, a directive ignored by the police and DA's office. The evening turned into a "happening", with the audience wildly cheering and applauding the attorneys, the author, the actors, and denouncing the civil authorities. After the performance there were speeches by invited celebrities, and the police left quietly. It was not until five days later that Berkeley also brought charges of "lewd and dissolute conduct in a public place."

After five months of litigation, Marshall Krause, of the ACLU persuaded the San Francisco Superior Court that the charges were inappropriate, and the case was dropped from court — an important legal precedent having been set. Following the San Francisco court action, the Berkeley court withdrew its charges. *Rare Angel Productions*, now free to perform *The Beard* in California, is resuming its production of the play.